IRAN
Tales of Persian

Stephen Platt

www.leveretpublishing.com

Iran: Tales of Persia
First published - June 2015
Second Edition - September 2017
Published by
Leveret Publishing
56 Covent Garden, Cambridge, CB1 2HR, UK

ISBN 978-1-9124600-5-2

© Stephen Platt 2015

All rights reserved. No part of this publication may be reproduced, stored in a retrieval system or transmitted in any form by any means, electronic, mechanical, photocopying, recording or otherwise, except brief extracts for the purpose of review, without the writ-

IRAN

Golestan Palace, residence of Qajar Shahs, rebuilt 1865, used for receptions till 1979

IRAN 2014 / 2015

TRIP 1: 2-30 January 2014

Tehran, Dizin, Manjil-Rudbar, Shiraz, Isfahan, Meybod, Chakchak, Yadz, Bam, Kerman

TRIP 2 14-31 May 2015

Nur and Caspian coast, Kuhdasht-e Kohan salt mine near Garmsar, Shahmizard, Badab Soort mineral springs, Choret Lake, Sari.

IRAN   January 2014

Thursday 2 January

I had five-hour layover in Istanbul. Instead of leaving the airport and finding the airport hotel I'd stayed in before, I found myself channelled into the long, chaotic queue for transit. This meant a five-hour wait in the departure lounge of Sabiha Gokcen airport.

I found a seat next to a Russian lady, called Irina, who told me her life story in Spanish. She was going back for her uncle's funeral in Siberia. He had drowned on a fishing trip to Lake Baikal. She was about fifty, blonde, with a ponytail. She left Russia with her husband after the Gorbachev revolution. They went first to Switzerland and then to Spain, where she now lived with her eldest son Dmitri and worked as a nurse. Her husband had run a bar in a town north of Barcelona, drank heavily and abused her. He had died of cancer, she said. Then changed her mind and said, no, he died at the hands of his Gypsy lover. I asked if he'd been involved in anything and she said, how did I know. He was a cocaine and heroin user and his lover had stabbed him in the neck in a fit of jealousy.

Mahdavi family - Abbas, Nesrin and Iman on holiday

Friday 3 January

I get through passport control and security with no problem. We take a taxi to Solmaz's flat and I have a sleep before Farnaz takes me to see the Golastan Palace – home of the Qajar Shars who had been deposed by Reza Pahlavi in 1925. The palace is now a museum. The first building is a museum of Persian culture and there mannequins dressed in traditional costumes and scenes of peasant life from different regions of Iran.

Golastan Palace garden

Edifice of the Sun (Shams ol Emareh)

Mirror Hall (Talar e Aineh)

Karim Khani Nook (Khalvat e Karim Khani)

It is Friday and the weekend so the streets are quiet and the Metro empty. We have hot chocolate and cheesecake in a favourite coffee house and, after going back to the apartment to change, we drive to Farnaz's home to meet her family – Nasrin, her mother, Abbas, her father, and Iman, her brother. Abbas is wiry with grey haired and has a moustache. He is nice, gentle and intelligent and has good English. Her mother is quiet and pretty under her headscarf. Iman is lovely. He has Down's syndrome and proudly shows me his medals for running. He is a keen soccer fan and likes the Liverpool shirt I brought him.

I hand out my presents, carefully wrapped in brown paper – a tea towel with an olive tree from the botanic Garden in Cambridge that goes down well as Nesrin's passion is her indoor plants which crowd the balcony. A notebook for Abbas. The present I bought for Sanaz's new baby I give to Iman by mistake which causes hilarity. For Farnaz I brought four bars of Green and Black's chocolate.

We sit around rather formally – me in my best suit. Farnaz's cousin Mohammad arrives. He is doing mechanical engineering and wants advice about doing a Ph.D. Imam takes me to his parents room shows me a trophy cupboard of his fretwork. Abbas explains that Iman goes to a special school. Will he be able to look after himself I wonder? Dinner is chicken, saffron rice, meat and spinach stew. There is delicious mushroom soup to start. Abbas apologises for no alcohol. I say it will do me good. I ask if their impression of England is that we are all alcoholic. They laugh, but obviously think so.

Abbas says he is supporting Farnaz but cannot pay for her Ph.D. studies. Maybe he disapproves of her wanting to do a doctorate. Mohammed says studying in the UK is too expensive and he is looking at Netherlands and the United States. He asks me where I would prefer. I say the country is less important than the institution and he should go to the best university he can.

Saturday 4 January
I awake at six and ready to leave by seven but there is heavy traffic. It is the first day after the holiday and we wait until 10 o'clock to leave. I sleep a lot on the way. Manjil is on the main highway north-west from Tehran. It is winter and the fields are bare grey stalks. There is a pall of pollution over Tehran so that the mountains are dimly seen. But the air is cleaner in Manjil and the sun is warm.

We find the only hotel in Rudbar, the next town north, which was also devastated. We venture forth and choose one of the many olive store owners to interview. He is about 50 and has lived all his life in the area. There is a coffee shop opposite the hotel. It doesn't serve coffee though, so we order tea and write up the notes from the interviews before Farnaz forgets. Then we go and do another round of interviews and so on.

Dinner is in a roadside restaurant that Ali Reza, Farnaz's brother-in-law recommended. It takes is a while to find in the dark because all she knows is that it is on the road between Manjil and Rudbar and is dirty. It's homely, and the cooking is good and wholesome. The hotel is rather basic and I have to repair the bed which sags in the middle.

Over view of Rudbar

Olive seller Rudbar

Tea shop in Manjil

Sunday 5 January

The following morning we drive round the town and up a dusty road into the mountains from where we can get an overview of the area. There are lots of settlements and villages high up, many of which were destroyed by landslides.

We stop in Manjil to find someone for brunch and find a delightful restaurant on the upper floor in the town square. Instead of tables and chairs there are raised carpeted booths. A couple of men are smoking shisha pipes. We have breakfast of tea and scrambled egg with tomato. There is snow on the high passes back to Tehran.

I spend the night at the Mahdavi's. They make me welcome and Farnaz's mother has cooked a lovely meal of soup, rice, green vegetable and meat stew, potato cakes and chicken with saffron.

Monday 6 January

In the morning I work with Farnaz applications doing PhD applications to Delaware and Pittsburgh.

That evening we meet Maryam and her brother Mohammed at the Steakhouse. We are a little late and they have arrived before us. Maryam is dressed in a bright yellow coat and obligatory headscarf. Most women here use heavy make-up and she looks quite different to how she looked back in the UK. She is pleased to see me and jumps up, smiling and laughing. Her brother is nice and smiles a lot and makes jokes.

Maryam says she plans to go to the States. Her brother says she won the lottery. I ask how much. They say you don't understand. There is an annual sweepstake for a Green card and she won. They say this was the last year they will be running the scheme. She intends to spend a year trying to get a job as an architect and making a new life. Maybe she hopes to find a man – it seems she is broken up with her fiancé. I am in humorous mood and entertain them with anecdotes. It's an enjoyable evening.

Tuesday 7 January

I stay at the Mahdavi's again because tomorrow we fly to Bam and have to leave at 6 am. Even at this hour there is heavy traffic with people trying to beat the rush. Abbas says four million people commute into Tehran every day, most by car. There are many complex highways and bridges. Iran must have invested heavily in road building some time in the recent past.

We reach the airport in good time. Men and women enter by different security gates. We reunite and go to check-in, but discover that the flight has been cancelled because of snow on the runway at Kerman. We have coffee and then make our way back home.

After breakfast we sally forth to change money and find an exchange near home and I get a thick wedge of notes for my thousand Euros. We then drive to Farnaz's bank and deposit the bulk of the money, keeping back £300 worth of Rial in cash for immediate spending, for example to hire ski gear tomorrow. Farnaz has opened a new bank account and has given me the card and yesterday we changed the security pin to my standard number.

We go for a late lunch at an Italian restaurant called Giovanni and share a Caesar salad followed by grilled prawns. There are various tables with groups of women, usually in threes that all look the same in their headscarfs and bright red lipstick. Farnaz says it's the surgery. They have all had the same nose jobs.

Wednesday 8 January

The forecast is for sun, but it's still dark when Farnaz comes to pick me up at six. We have a good run – most of the traffic is coming into Tehran. We go a long way west on the same highway before we can take the narrow single carriageway into the mountains to Dizin. The narrow the road winds through tunnels and sharp bends. We are following a bus that is driving fast but the cars still pass us. Farnaz is a great driver – confident and accurate and she loves going fast. She says when she was young she used to race boys and made a

Skiing at Dizin

Dizin

game of it. She says boys always think they are better drivers. She describes racing in the town and breaking every wing mirror of the cars parked in a narrow lane. She says people exchange phone numbers and meet up for coffee. Going to Manjil she played a game with another car when I was asleep and he paid our toll. This is the way people hook up here. In Tehran there are certain roads were the cars crawl along and people chat each other up.

We stop and ask a man who looks like a ski guide about hotels. He has a place and we take his number in case we stop over. The first hire shop is closed and we find another and I try various boots and get fitted out. It's sunny and cold and we have had to wait a little in the car park for the lift to start and join the lift queue. Farnaz says is much longer at the weekend.

The lift is a small gondola with four seats and we are joined by a woman who asked me, in English, where I'm from. She runs a gym. I ask how's business and she shakes her head wryly and says okay but she gets hassle from the police

I'm very rusty. The skis don't want to turn easily and the first slope is steep. I side-slip down until the slope eases. I'm really out of practice. Farnaz is solicitous but can shoot down at high speed. My legs ache and I wonder if I can cope. But we go back up and I manage to start turning properly with exaggerated weight shifting. We go all the way to the bottom this time and come up again and ski down to the middle station where there are restaurants.

We lie in the snow in the sunshine outside and chat, then go for a hot chocolate warm-up before skiing again. It's 3.30 before we go for lunch. I'm tired, my legs ache from the boots, but I start skiing properly and haven't

Skiing at Dizin

broken anything.

We nearly the last off the mountain and the guys in the ski-hire who have been so welcoming this morning are rather grumpy at being kept waiting. Farnaz passes me a neck pillow when she sees me nodding and I dozed until we are almost at the highway. Despite heavy traffic we have a good run back.

Farnaz's mother is ill with flu and Abbas has ordered a takeaway of rice and chicken. It is delicious after a long day. Again I sleep at the Mahdavi's.

Thursday 9 January
It is the weekend here and I expect Farnaz to get up late, but she wakes when I go into Iman's room to use the bathroom. She is sleeping on his floor while I use her bed. Abbas and I wait breakfast for her and all the family have breakfast together. We spend the morning working – Farnaz at her desk doing at TOEFL test and me on the bed doing the review a paper for the Disaster journal. It isn't easy because it's not very good.

We have arranged to meet Zhila, the woman I met in Dublin who works for the Institute of Earthquake Engineering and Seismology. We are running late so telephone and finally arrive about midday. She's very welcoming but when I offer to shake her hand after Farnaz she shrinks away. As we walk to her office she explains that there are cameras in the lobby. Farnaz whispers she could lose her job.

We have an animated discussion about recovery in Manjil and Bam. She specialises in social issues and is very informative. We have lunch in the director's office – rice and kebab. The director, plus one of his colleagues joins us and we have a wide ranging discussion - with me talking too much as neither of them seem to know much about economic recovery or urban planning. They seem eager to collaborate and want to invite me to a symposium in 2015. I describe the scenario planning exercise and they are interested. We finish and return to Zhila's office and Farnaz has a chat with her about living in Japan and careers in Iran. Zhila spent six years in Kobe and, like Farnaz, found it a lonely existence. She found the language difficult. Many Iranians earthquake specialists seem to have studied in Japan.

I managed to construct a detailed and helpful review and we post it. Then I concoct an email to Phil and Andy about the next board meeting and work on the abstract Abbas has written for a conference. I finish it and close it but it doesn't save as I've been working in the zipped version. It is frustrating and I'm amazed with myself. We break for lunch and I do it again after we have eaten.

It's late and we have arranged to meet Abbas's friend Mr Hassani. We drive to a hotel, the one I was meant to stay in before Solmaz offered me her flat. Hassani is waiting for us. He is fat jolly man in a brown suit. He likes taking centre stage and talks about his work on lifelines and his years in Japan. I ask if he has been to England and he catalogues all the countries he has visited. He relates his time in Japan as a young man. At some stage he goes to pray. Abbas says since the two universities amalgamated Hassani is his new boss. But only for a month or two since Abbas is retiring from teaching to continue his consultancy.

He says it is very expensive bringing up a family in Iran with sanctions because inflation is so high. He needs the money. I managed to get a word in and hold my own. I talk about the gas company in Istanbul and about scenario planning. He offers to hand on my questionnaire and send me some material. When we part in the street he gives me a strange double handshake, like the Masons. Maybe he just plays games Farnaz says later. She says he is arbitrary in the way he distributes patronage to young students. He said he would get her a job or a place to do a Ph.D. in a top university in Iran but she doesn't want to ask is help.

We go back home and I do my various jobs – emailing people I would like to interview to try and arrange to meet. When I tried to change my booking to a later flight I realise I've left my credit card at Solmaz's. We go back and get it. It doesn't take long but I'm worried that there are only five seats left. When we get back the booking page has expired so I repeat the process and manage to get the last seat. I find out where the Iranian embassy is and save the address on my phone. I finish all the jobs, collect my stuff and we drive to a fast food restaurant and have a hamburger washed down with fresh lemonade. It is midnight by the time I get to bed, having packed.

Friday 10 January
I wake five minutes before the alarm and am ready for the taxi at 3.30. The road is clear and we reach the airport in 40 minutes. I get through the various queues and buy a coffee and have a rest.

In Istanbul I get a taxi into town and get dropped at the embassy. It's all very easy, but I'm stupid and don't say I need it the same day so I waste time having to go to the bank twice. Never mind I still have time. The smiling clerk tells me to come back in an hour so I wander off in search of coffee. The embassy porter directs me but I find myself in the garment district – shop after shop of women's underwear, but no cafe. I give up and head back and, passing a men's shirt shop, I pop in and select a 100% cotton white shirt for €15 to wear at the weeding tomorrow. It seems a bargain. I ask the salesman about coffee and he says Starbucks. I say no, Turkish coffee. He suggests he make one in the shop. It's good.

I have to wait ten minutes but finally my visa arrives and I'm delighted, so delighted I don't pay attention when the clerk ostentatiously opens the page and shows me the visa. It is still early 10.30 and my plane isn't until eight in the evening so I head off on foot to the Sultanahmet – the Santa Sophia. It is as splendid as I remember.

I head from the sea and the Galata Bridge. I want to find the place by the sea at Karakoy where I had fried fish with Bahar. I stop and walk through an area of bookshops and handicrafts. I find a bench by the sea and watch the ferries plying back and forth for half an hour. It's sunny, but cold and I'm glad of my thick coat.

Halfway across the bridge a shoe-shine man drops his brush and I stop to tell him. He's grateful and offers to clean my shoes – in gratitude I think. When he's finished, talking about football and polishing my shoes, he asks for money. 25 Turkish Lira he says. I know it's too much. I should laugh and say no. But he has me at a disadvantage of reverse gratitude. I hand over 100 Turkish lira note

Santa Sophia Sultanahmet

Lunch on the waterfront

(about 40 USD). He has no change. He suggests he will get some from the cigarette seller. He dashes off leaving me his shoe-shine cleaning kit. I feel awful. I've just given him up and also given up thoughts of throwing his kit in the sea, when he reappears with my change having run from the bridge to the grand Bazaar and back. Somehow, bizarrely, my faith in human nature is restored!

The price of lunch by the waterfront is only 15 Turkish lira for a plate of fresh anchovy, salad, bread and water. Never mind the show cleaning fiasco, I got my visa, and lunch is delightful. I watch the world go by. The gulls fighting for scraps and the sunlight dancing in the water. The ferries run fast head on to the quay and fend off with a stack of tires on the bow. The captain holds it there on the engines while the passengers disembark and embark.

I walk north into a zone of maritime equipment – anchors, ropes, cleats and stainless-steel fittings. I cross the main road into an area selling sanitary ware. Shower fittings and toilet bowls spill out onto the footpath. I find the Galata funicular for a ride up the hill to a Istiklal Avenue. As usual it's thronged with promenading folk. I find a handy cafe but they have no water and so their loo is closed. I pass Turkish Cell and go in on an impulse to purchase a simm for my phone. I try ringing Iran when I'm back on the street but it immediately runs out of money. I go back and discover I've been registered for calls to Ireland not Iran. I pay more. Maybe it will work this time.

I head up the avenue and decide to go for the 4pm bus and find a cafe. I check my Visa and discover that it's only for eight days and I need fourteen to fifteen. I phone Farnaz and she says we have three options. I can go home early, I can stay in Turkey eight days or I can try and sort it out at the embassy and get a new Visa. All options seem equally unattractive. She doesn't like my suggestion of just turning up at the airport and hoping for the best because it may blacklist me.

I ring off and hurry for my bus. I assume I've missed it but in fact it's still there and about to leave. I ring Farnaz back and she suggests that I ring the embassy since it is still within working hours. She has already promised to ring the travel agency tomorrow. I get through to the same man and he recognises me. He is apologetic and was anticipating my call. He says he was surprised that the reference code only authorised eight days. I said what can I do? He said no problem – I can go to a police station in Iran and get an extension. I am annoyed with myself for not checking.

In the airport I find the Pegasus airline area but there was no-one there –

the flight is not for three hours. The machine allows me to print my boarding pass for the return but not for now. I ask for help and then realise in cancelling and rebooking my flight I had somehow booked myself on the 8pm flight yesterday not today. I had to go to the Pegasus desk and buy a new ticket. Again I hadn't been careful of the detail – a defect of character? I just have to try and make sure I don't lose anything.

I go from wash and shave find a coffee bar and have cheesecake, espresso and fresh lemonade. I plan to sleep on the flight, but then I am sitting between two nice looking women. One asks how long is the flight and the other contradicts me when I say an hour. She says it's only 55 minutes. I say thank God.

Her name is Hattie she's been living in Guildford with her boyfriend three years but has broken up and is on her way back to Izmir. She has a new boyfriend and is excited to meet him and his family. She studied fashion design but is in charge of rolling out a chain of stores in the Middle East.

I ask directions and find the Metro to the restaurant were I am to join the wedding party. Scharlie, Othman and Solmaz greet me at the station and we wait for the band to arrive on the next train. I am tired but I'm hungry and I enjoy the salad and sea bream. I fall asleep in the car back to Bahar's parents' home. Bahar has to guide me into the flat; I'm dead on my feet.

Bahar, Mustafa and Nursen

Saturday 12 January

We wake at eight and I dress in my casual gear and we go for breakfast in the restaurant across the road. It's a spread. Neil, his brother Mark and kids join us. The sun is shining. Bahar and Neil exchange rings. For them, they are married. I joke about weddings. That wedded means is an obsessive attraction to someone. I should keep my mouth shut.

We dress in our finery and sit around having our photos taken, waiting for Neil. It seems that his haircut and shave has taken longer than Bahar's hairdo and make-up. Then we go downstairs to the street. We nearly get left behind as I try to snatch a photograph of the bride and groom. Then the convoys sallies forth with hazard-lights flashing and horns blaring. Small boys run alongside to catch the bride's car and collect envelopes of money. Earlier Bahar's uncles have loaded her with gold bangles – another tradition.

The banquet is in a huge square room. We are on the same table as the band. We get talking with James, a young man in a pinstripe shirt, who works as a heritage archaeologist in London. An elegant blonde is sitting with us. She seems reserved. She's on her own and seems lonely. James talks to her but stops when he discovers she has a son.

We talk to her and find out that her husband has a construction materials business. Her name is Banu. She is animated and smiles a lot when talking. She says she does nothing and is bored. She would like to visit England with her family. I say to get in touch if she comes to Cambridge and give her my card. Solmaz and Işin are on another table. We eat – meze and then chicken and rice. I have white wine, then raki – it's strong. Then we dance. There is a Turkish

Işin and Solmaz

Neil, the groom

band. The lead singer, a woman, is very good.

Neill and Bahar are on their feet the whole night – circulating, meeting people and dancing. It's a great, huge public recognition of their marriage. At some point they put out a white table in the middle of the dance floor and the couple make their official vows. Then, a little late, a huge three-tier cake arrives and they cut it with a sword. Bahar prompts Neil to tip the waiter. He does and then offers money to Mustafa, Bahar's father. It's funny.

I dance with Scharlie and then Solmaz. Then the Red-stripe band play. They're a reduced combo – Costa on guitar, Ed and the saxophonist we saw in London. They are great and I cut loose with the dancing. I buy photo that the professional has taken. We are almost the last to leave since we're going with Mustafa and Nursen. Finally we are in bed and deeply asleep till late.

Sunday 13 January
We breakfast with the family. Bahar calls, solicitous as always. She spent her honeymoon night in a renovated Greek mansion in Força. They fly to Cappadocia tomorrow.

Mustafa and Nursen take us to the train and we have an easy journey to Istanbul. I have time before my late flight and go into town with Scharlie on the airport bus and help her find her hotel

We walk down the thronging Istiklal Avenue and I spot the cake shop 'Saray' that Bahar introduced me to. We have lentil soup, meatballs and rice and rice pudding. It's delicious. We continue down the avenue and pass the Galata Tower. This is the zone of music and musical instruments. The road narrows and steepens and then just before the sea we find the hotel down an alley on the left. It's perfect. Scharlie has a double and Nick and Helen have the Deluxe.

Scharlie walks back with me as she wants to explore the shops. I'm tired but stride out back up the hill to Taksim. I just miss the 7pm bus but catch the next one and get to the airport in good time and phone Farnaz over a beer.

Monday 14 January Tehran
I get to bed about 5.30 and sleep for two hours because today we have to extend my visa. We drive to the coach station and leave the car because it's an even day and we can't go into certain zones of the city.

There is a narrow entrance into the police station guarded by a uniformed cop. It's chaotic with lots of people milling about. But eventually I begin to sense some order. We get to see the chief. He's incredibly efficient. He listens, nods then signs or makes a note on the paperwork.

We go to the bank, get photocopies and have my photograph taken just down the street. Then we go back and have all our papers stapled into a pink folder and queue again to see the chief. He looks and signs and join the queue for the man dealing with visas. He says five days, come back. Oh dear!

Farnaz talks to a woman in the booth next to the chief's office. She seems to run the place. Farnaz explains we have a flight to Shiraz tonight. The woman says it's our problem. She is small in a black chador with spectacles. She looks formidable but Farnaz doesn't give up. "He is here to visit and see our beautiful country and if we have to wait five days he will lose all his time and money for flights and hotels", she says. The woman smiles and says she'll ask. She comes back after a short while and winks! My Visa is extended. We go back home and pack quickly and then take a taxi to the airport. Our flight is delayed but, finally, we get to our hotel after midnight.

Unfortunately the account of the next two weeks travelling in Shiraz, Isfahan, Yadz, Bam and Kerman was lost when my notebook was stolen in Alaska along with my computer. The following photographs give an impression of the trip.

Shiraz

Karimkhani Arg citadel

Bazar-e-Vakil

Faloodeh (famous Shiraz ice cream)

Naqsh-e Rustam

Bahar, Mustafa and Nursen

Tomb of Darius the Great

Tomb of Xerxes I

Persepolis

Gate of Xerxes or All Nations

Hall of 100 Columns

Bulls head capital

Persepolis

Faravahar Zoroastrian symbol.

Lion and bull in combat

Persian Immortals

Isfahan

Chehel Sotoun (Palace of forty columns)

Sheikh Lotfollah Mosque 'peacock' ceiling

Abbasi Hotel

Isfahan

Music hall Ali Qapu Palace

Armenian Vank Cathedral Julfa

Spice stall Isfahan Bazaar.

Isfahan

Masjed-e Shah courtyard

Naqsh-e Jahan Square

Coffee shop in Bazar

Isfahan

Pol-e Khaju bridge

Eating sour gharaghurut in Bazaar

Masjed-e Shah towards south Iwan

Kerman

Bagh-e Shahzdeh Prince's Garden

Our taxi driver from Bam to Kerman

Bagh-e Shahzdeh Prince's Garden

Meybod

Mud brick houses of Meybod

Water cistern ceiling in Caravanserai

Pigeon house

Yadz

Amir Chakhmaq Complex

Masjed-i Jamé mosque

Windcatcher House of Larry

Yadz

Qasim gymnastics club

Sweet shop

Street fruit sellers

Yadz

Windcatchers

Amir Chakhmaq Interior

Masoudi reservoir

Yadz

Late night bread making

Caesar restaurant

Tea house

Chakchak

Chakchak Ardakan fire temple

Cave with eternal fire and living spring

Road to Chakchak

Bam

Arg of Bam restoration after 2003 earthquake

Ruined date farm

Arg mason

Naqsh-e Jahan Square, Isfahan

IRAN

Badab Soort

IRAN   May 2015

Friday 15 May

I am sitting in a cafe in Istanbul, waiting for the Iranian embassy to open. I only found out two days ago that I was likely to get my visa. I had resigned myself to not coming – Jack, our grandson, is in hospital with leukaemia and Scharlie needs me at home. There were also things at work and it seemed the wrong time to go; in a way I was relieved. Then out of the blue an email arrived from the conference organiser saying I could collect my visa in Dublin. But I didn't have time; my only chance was to collect it on my way in Istanbul. I knew it was possible because I had done it the time before. I emailed them to ask them to give me a new number for Istanbul. I dithered and searched for flights, unsure how long I could stay away. I delayed 24 hours and the price went up £150.

    I rang the Iranian embassy in Istanbul to make sure that they had the permission. The clerk in the embassy was nice but reported, apologetically, that my number had not arrived. It usually takes 3 to 5 days, he said. When did you hear you got it? Yesterday I said, knowing it was now the weekend in Iran and the start of a holiday. I would lose my flight and not get to the conference. He could hear the alarm in my voice. Let me look again, he said and a moment later returned. Yes there is a fax. You can come tomorrow and collect your visa.

    Stansted was quiet for once, the plane full; but I slept. I left my bag in the airport and caught the bus to Taksim. I am used to this trip. I found a cafe for tea and a bread doughnut. I walk to the funicular down the hill to Kabataş. A helpful station guard changed my coin when the machine rejected it.

    I get off at the Gran Bazaar and follow my nose. I should have got off two stops later but never mind. I climb the hill, tired from lack of sleep and hot in the morning sun. And then there it is, the embassy, and the bank in front where you pay. And now I'm drinking bad coffee waiting for 8.30 when it opens. It all went very smoothly after a short anxious wait because he couldn't find my number in the file. Then relief when he found the fax.

    I wander around the garment district, trying and failing to find the shirt shop I used before. It was more crowded when I got back. The majority people seem to be young men pleading for a visa for new brides. Disappointment again that the visa was only for six days! The man gave an apologetic shrug – that's all they authorised, he said. But I know I can try and get an extension like last time.

I caught the tram back. It was warm in the sunshine and I stopped by the sea and had a cheese toasty and yoghurt drink. Then the funicular to Taksim and a walk through the park to the bus. It's a nice park: it would be criminal to build a shopping mall over it. This place is symbolic so maybe it would be a step too far for the Erdoğan government.

I sleep on the bus, collect my case from left luggage and walk over to the hotel. It is such a luxury being able to stay here. Only 100 yards away and very pleasant. I wake bleary eyed but refreshed; shower, dress, clear the room and check out. Then a leisurely dinner in the hotel restaurant - chicken kebab, chips and an Efes beer. I slept most of the flight. I was set next to a girl from London. Her parents Iranian. Her father was a lawyer and had come to Britain before the revolution. She had decided at the last minute the day before to come to her cousin's wedding. They had been childhood friends. He was marrying an Iranian girl. I don't know why, she said. He had pleaded with her to come. She hadn't wanted to because she hated Iran, mainly, I think, because of the way it treats women. She had studied pharmacy but found her job consisted of labelling packages of medicine. So she had set up her own business as a beautician.

Taksim, Istanbul

ISG Hotel. Sabhia Gokcen airport

Saturday 17 May

There were long queues for passport control. There were three queues for foreigners and it wasn't clear which one was moving quicker. The man on my queue seemed to take an endless time checking. Finally all the booths for Iranians cleared so I tried one and was sent away by a rather fierce black-shrouded young woman. Feeling foolish and not wanting to return to my original line I tried another young man with better luck.

There was a scrum to get through the baggage check at the customs control and then I was in the arrivals hall looking for Farnaz. I couldn't find her and it turned out she had been waiting in another entirely different arrivals. It had taken a while, but I was more fortunate than a party of four elderly French who had hoped to get their visas on arrival and were still being interviewed.

We caught a taxi, the roads were empty and we were soon at the Mahdavi's apartment in Pasdaran. I had a long sleep and then we went for lunch at a nice restaurant round the corner: a vegetarian place with a courtyard garden. We shared a salad and spinach calzone and I had dough, a spiced yogurt drink.

Abbas and Iman arrive and cook chicken and rice. After they have gone to bed Farnaz takes me on a walk around the neighbourhood to help me get my bearings for tomorrow – I plan to go to the currency exchange where I changed money last year. We walk to the main avenue in Pasdaran and have

Ananda vegetarian restaurant.

Ekhtiyarieh, Behestan, Pasdaran

fruit drinks – banana milk for me and melon for Farnaz. Then to a very flat, hard bed in Iman's room that he has kindly vacated for me.

Sunday 17 May

I woke and just had time to say goodbye to Abbas and Farnaz before they left for work. I grabbed a quick breakfast of bread and cheese washed down with tea and got to my desk. I pinch Farnaz's chair, because Iman's is too hard, and work on the book chapter I'm writing. It was due last Thursday, the day I left, so I'm overdue.

At eleven I make coffee and then venture forth to change money. The roads are crowded today. I checked the rate online and expect to get 22 million Rial. Since they offer me 25 million I consider it a good deal. They couldn't transfer the money to the card Farnaz has given me so I again leave with a thick wodge of notes.

I get back into the flat and do another hour's work before warming up leftovers from last night for lunch. I work again until five. I have been a little discouraged with the work on recovery. I have been too ambitious. It is a huge field and I get confused about where I'm up to, what I've done already. But I devote a couple of hours to making lists and felt better.

Garden of Mahmood Hesabi, a famous Iranian scientist

The evening we go for tea in the garden of Mahmood Hesabi, an Iranian scientist and founder of the University of Tehran. There were beautiful trees and running water and sculptures of iconic buildings, but the food isn't great.

Monday 18 May
I got up with the alarm. I could have slept more. After breakfast, Farnaz's mother and I caught a taxi to where the website said we would find the police station for foreigners. It was the same place as last year but unfortunately the man on the gate said it had moved so we had to drive back across town to the east. The driver chatted the whole way with Nasrin perhaps explaining the various tortuous routes he takes to avoid traffic jams.

Although the venue had changed I recognise the same woman in a chador from last year and the swarthy police chief in charge, saying little and writing neatly on my form. He gives us a nod and sends us over to the detectives' room. A young man in civvies listens to Nasrin's story and smiles a lot. Then a rather diffident man arrives, asking permission to intrude and have a word with the young man. He sits at the other desk and chats to Nasrin. Meanwhile he flicks through my passport carefully, hovering over the various visas and stamps. I have three from Iran, one for Columbia, China, Pakistan, USA, and many for Turkey. Then in perfect English he ask, Why are you here? For a conference, I say. On what? Earthquake engineering. Where is it? The Milad Tower. Have you an invitation letter? No I never got one.

He does some phoning and a lot of checking on his computer. He makes phone calls. I learn later that he doesn't think I'm going to a legitimate conference at all. He speaks to Farnaz and then Zhila, who is a little brusque with him. The nice woman in a chador from last year comes with a bag of bananas and offers each of us one. It's slightly surreal. Then she brings me a plate and the younger detective nods to me to eat.

How long do you want? Until 2 June. Fifteen days would be more flexible. He nods. It seems settled. He makes notes in his computer then we are back in the system registering my photos with the same young man in uniform who staples all the forms together in the pink folder. I join the queue to leave my passport and find that I've forgotten to fill in one of the forms in duplicate. Finally we are finished and back with a taxi driver who waited for us. We stop on the highway to let Nasrin out and I carried on to the conference.

I met Kambod, the conference organiser, soon after I arrived and he took me to register and get my name badge. Then I went to find my lecture room, in the bowels of the fourth basement. I am imagine no one else will find it and I will be lecturing to an empty audience. It was locked, so I went back up to the foyer and found a sofa and bought a Red Bull to wake me up.

I work on my laptop rehearsing my talk and changing a couple of the slides. Then Zhila turned up and introduced me to her friend and we go for lunch. Her friend is an electrical engineer. Zhila asks how Jack is doing and I explain. Then the friend starts telling me about an American woman who has written a book about natural treatment for cancer. I listen politely for a long while but she was very insistent I get a copy of the book. I try to tell her gently I am not interested but she won't stop. She says it wouldn't hurt to know and knowledge is good thing. Finally I lose patience with her and tell bluntly that I was not interested. She is shocked. Jack was diagnosed suddenly last Christmas, I say. It was a terrible shock. His parents had to act to save his life. They decided on a course of treatment with his doctors and began at once. Any other alternative treatment, if I were to suggest now, would imply they had made the wrong decision. That is not what they need at the moment. They need love and support and to believe that the very best is being done for their son. Zhila leapt in to say I was right. I felt I had been too hard on her. Oh well! Then it was time to find the loo and go to give my lecture.

I am co-chairing the session and a young man arrives breathless and introduces himself. His English is good. He is interested in talking to Robin: he'd heard we had a database of building stock. I said I'd introduce him but I couldn't promise anything. We were a commercial company not a government research institute or university and our data is our intellectual property.

People begin to arrive, including various of the international delegates. I feel pleased I have such a good audience. We begin fifty minutes late. I introduce the session briefly and go to the podium to give my talk. I am using my own computer because their version of PowerPoint lacks a presenter view. It turns out to have been a mistake. The colours on my slides are all washed out. When we get to the slides of remote sensing I have to apologise because it was impossible to see the colours. Then the projector begins to fail completely. Kambod shouts from the back that the connection is loose and I will have to hold it in. So I give the lecture holding the video plug into the side of my laptop. It is uncomfortable and ungainly but at least the colours show up.

There are a couple of nice questions – one from a Norwegian about whether disasters might be a catalyst for improvement and another from Kambod about speed and the quality of new housing in Turkey.

We are onto the other speakers. My co-chair is good and gets us back on track with the timing and thanks to one speaker not turning up we finish almost on time.

I go with Zhila to find a taxi and she introduces me to Ashtiany, the founder of the Institute who is standing in the lobby. A taxi had just pulled up. Zhila looks doubtful but I climb in and she gives the driver my and we say goodbye.

I get home before the traffic. Farnaz, Iman and I drive to the Enghelab golf course in central Tehran. Pooyan, Farnaz's boyfriend, is waiting for us. He asks if I can walk. I say, yes I can still walk, wondering if he's having a crack at my age. It's 2.5km! he says.

The walk is a rectangular track 4m wide bounded by high wire fences and poplar trees. Two lanes are marked out and people are walking in both directions – some in sports clothes and others not. It is dark and quite pleasant walking along with Iman. We encourage each other and keep pace with the couple in front. We leave Farnaz and Pooyan far behind. They want to talk. They are almost engaged. The problem is that no one in Pooyan's family will stand up for him when he comes to see Abbas, Farnaz's father and mother.

Pooyan's parents are separated. He lives with his mother and supports her. His younger brother, who is only 18, still lives with his father. Somehow Pooyan got himself through college and to Sharif University, one of the best universities in Iran, without much help from his family. They were in the States during his high school years so his English is good. But neither his father nor his mother will with him. Maybe his mother doesn't want him to leave her. So he talked to his uncle, his mother's brother, who was nice to him and bought him dinner, but wouldn't go against his sister. So why not to go alone, I wonder.

Pooyan is interesting. He is sarcastic and maybe has been a little rude the two times with met. Farnaz says he doesn't like people. He likes to be alone with her and doesn't like going out with her friends. The question Farnaz is asking herself is whether he can change or whether he's too big a challenge. She likes many things about him. He's clever, hard-working and resourceful. He's had to look after himself a lot – feeds himself and washes his own clothes. This is made him very independent. But his diet is suffered. He only eats pizza with pepperoni or hamburger. His health has suffered. He quit smoking a few months ago and is putting on a little weight. Of course all this could change in a loving household. But he is also very self-contained and distrustful of people. This makes him self-centered.

He works every night till nine giving classes at an English Language Institute. The money is good for Iran. He recently went to Dubai for an interview with Slumberger who offered him a job in Iraq starting in September and if they marry Farnaz will probably join him. So her life could totally change, from a Ph.D. in Canada or North Texas to a housewife in Iraq. I think they're brave; I imagine Iraq as a dangerous, god-forsaken war zone. But Iraq is Iran's closest neighbour, part of what was once the same empire.

We are halfway round the circuit. I'm a little bored, thinking about Caracas and comparing it with Tehran. They are both big, throbbing cities separated from the sea by high mountains. And both, interestingly, have an earthquake risk. Of course there are many differences.

I remember my life there arriving with my suitcase having been stolen, frightened and with the frightening responsibility of having to find a place for my family and make a living. I think about Pooyan and how he's feeling. I can see why Farnaz is having trouble with her decision. I can't decide about him either. Sometimes I think he's a good and at other times I wouldn't want anything to do with him.

We are on the down strait now, painted signs on the roadway tell us we've done 1800m. I speculate about the dark place beyond the high wire fence. It must be the golf course. That's why the fences so high, I guess. Iman is tired so we stop and let Farnaz and Pooyan catch up. They are deep in talk.

We set off again and reach the cafes at the start of the walk and go and buy drinks. We sit on a low wall and talk. We somehow get into talking about medical advances. Maybe we were talking about Jack and his leukaemia or maybe about biotech in Cambridge or maybe we were talking about elites and the rich and I had made a comment about how it was good that the rich can't take it with them. Anyway Pooyan says he doesn't understand why people want to prolong life, because life is so awful. I say he might not think the same when he's my age.

Pooyan abruptly says I need to take Iman for a walk so Iman and I go and sit on a wall to watch the people walking by. Farnaz and Pooyan are in heated discussion. Finally, we leave and drive to a place to have dinner. It is nice with tables next to a pool. The food is good. Pooyan is a little more relaxed. I make an effort. We talk about Scotland and happiness. I said you paid last time, so it's my turn. That's how you Brits do it, he says. Sure I say. He looks pleased.

Tuesday 9 May

Kambod had invited me to a UN VIP session that began at 8.30. So I leave the house early and have an easy run. Professor Ashtiany, gives a talk about the new Sendai framework. Yesterday, when Zhila introduced me, he told me how he had been refused a UK visa even though he had arranged a meeting with someone in the Cabinet office. Then a young Iranian woman from UNISD gave an extremely lucid talk on a similar theme. Then a third speaker from UNESCO, a Greek, gave a rather poor speech. Finally Kambod gave a talk. It was supposed to be a round table discussion but there wasn't much time for the panel so, although I had prepared something to say, I kept my mouth shut.

There was a second session after coffee but I'd had enough and decided to head back home to work. I sat down in the foyer to collect my things and was suddenly startled by a couple I'd met the day before. They were a man and wife team who said they were making a TV documentary about foreigners

Interviewed by Saeedeh at the conference

and their attitudes to Iranian culture and cuisine. They had asked me if they could interview me. I had said yes and had given them my card. Now they had caught me off-guard. I jumped up looking for somewhere else to be interviewed. I felt exposed right in front of the main entrance.

I feel come uncomfortable here, I said. Why, he asked. It feels too low on the sofa. We can go somewhere else. Never mind we can do it here, I say. I sit back down on the sofa and try to relax as the young girl who is the interviewer sits next to me. She has a clipboard with questions. Her English is good. Is this your first time in Iran, she asks. How do you find it? Why are you here? Where have you been? Do you like the food? What food? Racking my brains I say I like breakfast, it's so much more interesting than in the UK. I wanted to talk about the Persian stews but I can't remember what they are called. What you think of hijab? I have no comment about hijab. It's a different culture and I respect people's right to choose. Where are you staying? What do you think about the conference? And so on. I ask if I can have a copy if they make a film. I would like to put it on our website, I say. We finish the interview. I have done well in not saying anything I might have regretted. I say goodbye and go to find a taxi.

Wednesday 20 May.
Farnaz's session was first thing. We had stayed up late the night before rehearsing. We again had an easy run and arrived early. Having found the room we find a sofa and go through the slides and make final changes. Just before we were due to start Farnaz went to the toilet. When she got back the chairperson, Yasmin, was still waiting for people to turn up. I forgot my phone, says Farnaz in alarm. Go get it, I say.

I am worried she won't get back in time but she is back just after we start. The first two papers are about teaching earthquake awareness to kindergarten children. The first speaker is quite forceful but had no English and her slides are poor. Yasmin does her best to translate. She is co-author and suggests she deliver the second half of the talk to save time but the speaker has none of it.

Each speaker should have been allotted 15 minutes according to the programme. But the first paper took 45. The second paper is even worse. At questions a man at the back voices exactly what I have been thinking. Does this training have any meaning, he asks. Does it make children safer? Or is the problem that the schools will collapse and telling children to crawl under flimsy tables is creating a false impression that something has been done about their safety.

Then the Norwegian professor says teachers could help save injuries in minor quakes and that it was worthwhile. It was threatening to turn into a free for all. I can see Farnaz is getting increasingly agitated. There are 30 minutes left, supposedly for five speakers. So I put my hand up and say, it is not my place, but I am concerned that there will be no time for the remaining speakers. Yasmin thanks me and we move on to a speaker from Pakistan called Ghazala Naeem talking about tsunami risk in the Gulf and an event in 1947 that killed 4,000 people. I recognised her from Alaska. I met her one rainy evening at a conference dinner in the Eskimo Heritage Centre. Her talk was interesting and I wondered if the tsunami risk extended to Iran.

Farnaz is on. I get the video camera out and hold it steady. She is clear and confident and speaks well. People find it interesting. There are lots of questions. It turns out fine as Farnaz is the last speaker – three people have failed to turn up. Maybe Yasmin knew it but it would have been helpful if she had said something.

We go to tea because Farnaz wants to meet a friend from Japan. I talk to Ghazala. She remembers me. I tell her I had my bag stolen and had lost the

Farnaz giving her paper at the conference

card she gave me and that's why I hadn't contacted her before. She asks if I have finished the chapter on Pakistan. I say no. She says she is waiting for me. She introduces me to her colleague – the director-general of meteorology in Pakistan and we talk about tsunami risk and the possibility of collaboration. He said you have my card.

We set off. I am descending the stairs ahead of Farnaz who is saying goodbye to her Japanese friend when I run into the girl who interviewed me yesterday. When are you leaving Tehran, she asks. At the end of the month I say. Good, she says, would you like to be my friend? Farnaz comes and I introduce them. Do you live in England, Saeedeh asks. Why do you ask? say Farnaz. You were speaking English. I'm sorry we have to go, I apologise. Farnaz has to go to work and I need to collect my passport from the police station. Stupidly I put out my hand. I can't shake, she says.

We take separate taxis. My driver is a woman. She is a good driver, precise and efficient. I fall asleep. I awake when we stop and she says we are there. I'm bleary eyed. She smiles and points to the police station. I cross the road blinking sleep away and pass the police porters and climb the stairs and queue for my passport. It's ready and they have given me until June 5. Longer than I needed. I am pleased. I knock on the door to the detective's room. The man who interviewed me is there. There's no need, he says. I was just doing my job. Imam Ali said we have to help foreigners. I know you are just doing your job, I say, but I want to thank you anyway. He is pleased and we shake hands. I walk back to the car. The driver is pleased I'm pleased.

We go back a different way, down narrow streets, but it is very efficient because we reach the main avenue only one street away from where the Mahdavi's live. I didn't know how much money she was asking for so I handed her my wallet. She smiles and counts out what she needs. She seems to try and touch my hand as she hands back the money. But I pull away not wanting to offend her. Relations between men and women are supposed to be very formal here. But she touches her lips and blows kisses. I smile back and grab my things. She blows me more kisses as I climb out. Wow, I think as I skip across the avenue between the lines of traffic. I get on with some work at my desk waiting for Farnaz to get home from work.

We packed the car quickly and set off the new holiday house in the north on the Caspian coast. We stopp at the grocers on the corner to buy nuts, chocolate and drinks for the journey. We expect it to take four hours.

Although it wasn't a holiday there was a lot of traffic, but at least it was moving freely. We headed east on the highway before turning north towards the mountains. The road is narrow and winding, the scenery dramatic. The mountains are dry and the rock is unbelievably loose. These are such young hills. In the valley bottom there are splashes of green where there is water. Finally we are there. Again we stop at the corner shop. The few tomatoes they have are past their best but we buy yoghurt, olives and cheese. Farnaz says there is bread in the fridge which we can defrost on the gas ring. We also buy cappuccino. We boil a kettle and have a picnic before going to bed.

Thursday 21st of May
Despite being tired we wake reasonably early. We only have one day. We have breakfast on the terrace with the same ingredients as last night and venture forth. Farnaz has heard about a dam and lake that are worth visiting. There are pedal boats in the form of swans. It looks like hard work because it's windy. So I suggest we walk a little before boating. Young people ride horses and bicycles along the lakeside or race around on quad bikes. Farnaz wants a go on one.

We reach the end of the lake where there is a dirt road winding up through the trees that encourages us to explore. Three men are lighting a fire to make

Mahdavi's house near Caspian Sea

Living room

tea and have spread a carpet on the forest floor to spend the afternoon. Music is playing from the open door of their car. They invite us to join them, but we smile and carry on.

The track reaches a forest road and we turn uphill. We walk for an hour, steadily rising with views of the dam and the villages on the Caspian Sea. Suddenly Farnaz stops. We have disturbed a large brown snake, thick in the body with a big triangular head, that has been set sunning itself by the side of the dirt road. It slithers beautifully across the road and into the undergrowth. We give it a wide berth since it is likely to be venomous. We walk on for a while. We haven't reached anywhere, but Farnaz is tired and wants to turn back.

We pass the three men on their rug, smoking shisha and see no more snakes until we get back to the lake. We hear screaming. A man has caught a small water snake. It is brown, like the other one, but quite different, being thin delicate. The man holds it by the tail and waves it at the children, who run away screaming. I am upset, thinking he will kill it for fun.

We go on and have tea in the teashop on stilts sticking into the lake. We sit at the only table near the water and the man brings a pot of tea with cakes, dates, cucumber, apple and nuts that were difficult to eat. We sit for an hour or so chatting. It was nice. We mainly talk about Pooyan. Farnaz wants to

Dam above Nur

know what impression I have formed of him. I say I still don't know him well enough to say.

From there we drive to a hotel on the beach and have surprisingly good cappuccino in the cafe on the pier. After we walk along the beach. The sky and sea are grey today. Like an Irish Sea beach on a grey day. But we enjoy walking on the sand and chatting.

We walk back to the shops and Farnaz asks if I'd like to get anything for Scharlie in an expensive gift shop. Sure, I say and let's get something for your mum too. Farnaz said her mother liked this shop. Farnaz pointed out things her mother had admired – painted serving dishes for nuts or sweets and painted bowls on stalks. I finally settle on a glass cake dish with a glass domed lid for Nasrin and a glass candle-holder and soft red candles for Scharlie. Not to be outdone, Farnaz spots a mug with a lid that she could have at the office for coffee.

On the way Farnaz rang Ali Reza for advice about where to eat and we drive along the coast for a while asking directions until we find the place he recommends. It is a collection of fast-food outlets and not very nice at all. It doesn't matter.

Caspian Sea

Friday 22 May

We get up early and again have breakfast on the terrace and pack quickly. I see more of the road going back and we stop to take photographs. We have come back early to go to a leaving party for Farnaz's cousin who is emigrating to the United States to join her sister in Columbus, Ohio. She is a graphic designer and got her green card because of her artistic ability.

It is a big family gathering. I sit next to an uncle. He is quiet and nice and has good English. We speak about international relations. He has been in England. Everyone is very friendly and I feel relaxed. I am introduced to more people. I talk to a young man in his early thirties. He complains about not being able to find work.

We go into lunch. I sit at the table and the uncle helps serve me. I start with the thick bean soup – so thick it was almost a stew. I really like it. Nasrin looks pleased; she'd made it. I decline the chicken and have rice and salad. I also skipped the two puddings – chocolate blancmange and a green marble jelly set in a traditional jelly mould form. Back in the sitting room, I talk to Abbas. It is all very relaxed and pleasant and I think what a privilege it is to be with the family like this and see the country through their daily lives.

Some of the family will go to the airport tomorrow morning at 4 am to see her off. People leaving the old for the new. We get home and Farnaz changes

Route 77 Haraz Road back to Tehran

quickly in the toilet in the parking – whipping off the maroon silk top she has been wearing for the party and on popping on a blue one. Pooyan is coming to speak to her father a week on Monday and they have a lot to talk about.

Saturday 23 May

First thing we went to renew Farnaz's passport. I wait in the car and write my journal. Then we drive to her work down a leafy cul-de-sac off a highway. I walk back. It is straightforward but soon after I start down the main road the footpath runs out, so I turn left and find a quiet side street running parallel to the highway. I cross over Dolat and find a series of linking alleys running parallel to the main road. There were lots of trees and welcome shade. It is very pleasant. I get back home in half an hour and set to work on my chapter. I can't believe how long it's taking me. After Farnaz got home and had a brief rest we went out to the Ab Va Atash park (meaning fire and water, a Zoroastrian idea) to meet Pooyan.

We park and wander into the park. We dawdle on the bridge until it gets dark, taking photographs and then crossing to the park and wandering through the trees. We get a call from Pooyan to say he has arrived and we go back and meet him on the bridge.

The road back to Tehran

We drop down a level to where there are cafes. Pooyan asked what I'd like to eat. I said hamburger, knowing he likes them. You like this kind of place he asked. Not really, I said. Why? It's a fast food place. Really? That's what we call it. We do too, says Pooyan.

The hamburger isn't great and I wish I had kept Farnaz company and ordered a salad. Pooyan gets very passionate, explaining that Farnaz doesn't understand him. Later, after we had got to the cars and said goodbye, Farnaz said he never did that. She liked it, that he got so passionate. Usually he is indifferent, saying what was the point of arguing because you couldn't change anything.

Sunday 24 May

Today I go for lunch at the Institute with Zhila and we chatted for a while about different ideas for projects, then an elderly man in a white jacket brought lunch – chicken and rice. I ate about a third. There was a map on the wall and I asked about Iranian geography. I learned that during the Iraq war, which lasted much longer than I had thought, missiles regularly fell on Tehran and that troops had invaded deep into Iranian territory. I also learnt about different tribal areas and ethnic groups – Turkmen, Baluchi, Kurd, Lorestan. I also learnt that there was an ongoing Sunni insurrection in the south-east in

Leafy alleys (side roads) of Tehran

the area between Kerman and the Pakistan border.

Zhila orders me a taxi and when I get home I type up my notes and email them back for the meeting with Institute heads on Tuesday.

That evening we went to the Milad Tower to use the two free tickets I got at the conference. The tower is a concrete spire 432m high with a large pod three-quarters of the way up with restaurants.

We circle round the pod, taking photographs of the city. And then Farnaz has a long phone call with Pooyan but refuses to see him because he is still working till nine every night despite her asking him to finish early some nights so they can see each other.

Monday 25 May

I work all day again on my chapter and in the evening we go out for Farnaz to buy a present for Scharlie. We go to the jewellery quarter. The first shop we try is modern and Farnaz is tempted by a leather orange bangle with a gold clasp. But she decides to try another shop and settles on a brown bead bangle, again with a gold clasp. People really like gold jewellery here; it is almost like a family nest egg to be sold to get over difficult patches. It's an ancient idea of storing wealth in a country where paper money loses value so quickly. I leave Farnaz to negotiate and wander into a piano store. The saleswoman leaps up.

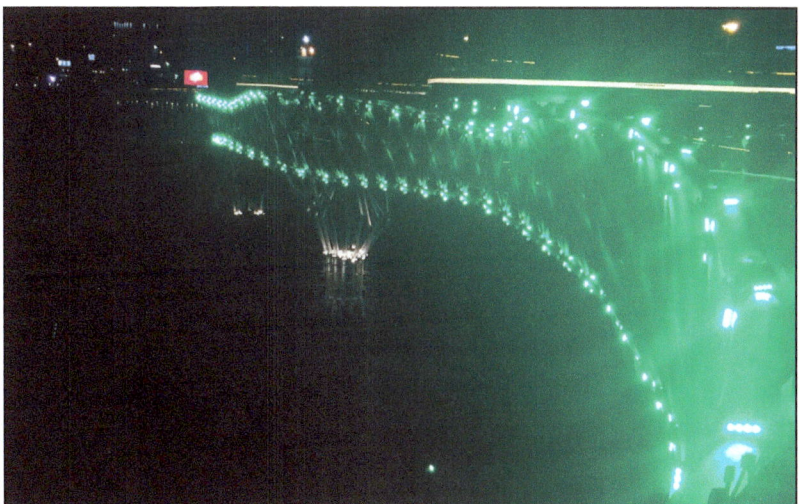

Bridge in Ab Va Atash Park

Maybe I'm her first customer today. I back out apologetically.

We ring Ali Reza again for advice about where to eat. I fancy traditional Persian. He recommends an expensive restaurant called Shandiz. We have a job finding it but as usual adopt Farnaz's tried and trusted method of asking directions of any likely passing person. The restaurant is old-fashioned and the food very good. We had tenderloin with rice. But to start there was an abundant salad bar with all manner of tempting dishes and the crusty bread I like. Many of the other diners look rather religious, the women wearing the black coverall and headdress.

Tuesday 26 May

Today begins like every other day with family breakfast around the table. Abbas is usually first and gets the bread and lays the table. It's comforting listening to the soft murmurings of quiet conversation. Iman is first to leave. His mother makes a sandwich – spreading cheese on the bread and folding it into a roll to keep him going mid-morning since he doesn't get back for lunch till after two. Then Farnaz rushes to her room, throws on a scarf and rushes off to work.

I am due to go to the institute but have to wait for a call or email from Zhila

Milard Tower

to tell me when Dr Jafari, the President, is available. He made a joke when I met him after the conference dinner. I told him I was staying with someone he knew – Abbas Mahdavi. He said I see, free accommodation!

I worked all morning then Abbas made me lunch. I got a call saying the meeting was at three. It was an easy ride and I arrived early and Zhila and I chatted about family, and about the ideas we had listed as potential projects. The first builds on their ideas from previous work about vulnerability in Iran and the second about recovery in Bam and Manjil. One of the proposals was a little unusual –tsunami risk in the Makran region in the south of Iran near the Gulf of Hormuz. I had found two papers suggesting tsunami here was more likely than had been thought. I was pushing this idea because it built on Farnaz's work on evacuation in Japan and also because I Ghazala, the Pakistani woman I met at the conference, had given a paper about the 1947 tsunami and its impact in Pakistan. I thought the Institute might be interested in a collaborative project with Pakistan.

We went up a floor to the small conference room I had been in last year. Reza arrived and asked if we should start or wait for Dr Jafari. I said let's wait, so he started the meeting anyway. He was particularly keen on building vulnerability and casualty modelling and wanted to work with CAR. Kambod came and gave me a friendly hello and asked after Jack. Then Dr Jafari arrived

View of Tehran looking south from Milard Tower

and we got down to business. There are six ideas here, he said. We only need one. They build on your previous work and we can decide which one or two you want to focus on, I said.

We talked about the tsunami risk and they dismissed it. Kambod was keen I focus on community preparedness and communication given my background. Zhila said we could and that I was interested in risk perception. I said it would be interesting to see how people's perception of risk mapped onto the hazard maps they had for Tehran. Dr Jafari said it was problematic working in the capital for security reasons. But maybe if the project went ahead we could work in a suburb to the west. But for now there was no need to say where we would work. I realised Dr Jafari is a typical engineer: practical, focused and pragmatic.

The discussion moved on to funding and the possibility of getting European funds. I felt ill-prepared. I should have sorted this before I came. I talked about the World Bank. While there are still sanctions, said Dr Jafari, there was no chance World Bank funding. Kambod talked about contacts in UNISDR and the VIP meeting last week at the conference. It seems promising and they also like the idea of collaboration with Turkey and Pakistan.

They made it clear that they had no funds for research and that the government was cutting back on spending. I said CAR had no research funds either. What kind of car is it then, asked Jafari, a Ferrari? More of a bicycle, I say. But we could pump-prime some research and get started, I say. What's pump priming? I explain about the water needed to get started. How much water are we talking about asks Jafari. Not a lot I say.

We shook hands and said goodbye. Kambod said he was surprised, given all the visa trouble, that I had managed to come. I said I was very tenacious.

I got back home and told Abbas I had arranged with Farnaz to walk round to her work with Iman. He looked a little worried. By taxi, he asked. No walking. Iman doesn't know the way. I do, I said, I walked back one morning. Okay take my number he says.

Iman wore his best clothes. Rather than take the alleys like last time, I decided to walk along the main roads. It wasn't as bad as I expected as there were some shade and the traffic pollution wasn't at all bad.

I held Iman's hand when we crossed roads. He lagged behind, so I waited for him. It was a climb up the main highway and I wanted to go the side route. But I also wanted to check if Farnaz was right that the footpath really went all the way. She was right; there was just a short stretch of about 30m where you had to balance on the curb. It was hot in the strong sunshine and Iman found it difficult balancing. Later he told Farnaz it was dangerous. But we made it and got to Farnaz's work at five on the dot.

We found some shade and chatted to Farnaz's auntie who was waiting to collect her daughter who also worked in the same place. Farnaz drove us to the park she had wanted me to see the other day. It was bigger and much nicer than I'd imagined from my brief view from the car. There was running water, beautiful trees and lots of benches with people sitting and chatting or wandering along the paths. Farnaz said she used to come here with her first serious boyfriend. They used to come here when they were in high school, to use the library and revise. One day, she said, they were walking here hand-in-hand when she saw her parents with Iman. They saw her at the same time. My parents! she cried. The boyfriend ran off. The parents said nothing about it but sometime later they invited the boyfriend to the house and Abbas told him he had to behave himself or he would be in deep trouble.

We reach the top of the park and go out to find the ice cream shop. It is wonderful. I have a cone with hazelnut and a tub with coffee mocha. Iman really liked it and went back for a second scoop. It is very popular and lots of young people came in.

We finally left and Iman said he needed the toilet so we try to hurry. Not

Sanaz and Ali Reza

in these shoes, he said. I like them, I said. You can have them, I give them to you he said!

We drive home, had a quick rest then go to Sanaz's and Ali Reza's for dinner. Nasrin has had Taha for the day and we are taking him home. There is no seat in the car so I hold him tightly. He is very good and lets me hold him. Sanaz and Ali Reza are very welcoming. I have a vodka and coke – the first alcohol I've had since I arrived. They serve beans and bread and yoghurt. I have too much not realising there is a main course to follow.

Taha is delightful. He likes me and we play ball. He's only 18 months old and still small but he's very active and very cute and intelligent. Abbas and Nasrin dote on him. Abbas rolls around the floor with him and Nasrin talks baby talk with him. He loves staying with them and is their first grandchild. When I came last they were very worried about Sanaz's health and whether she would have a successful birth.

The main course is puréed potato in my honour, with chicken and salad. There is a football match on with Ali Reza's favourite team, Persepolis. But they aren't very good, so I get bored and play with Taha. Finally it is time to leave. Ali Reza gives us detailed directions for our road trip tomorrow and lends us his camping gear in case we can't find somewhere to stay.

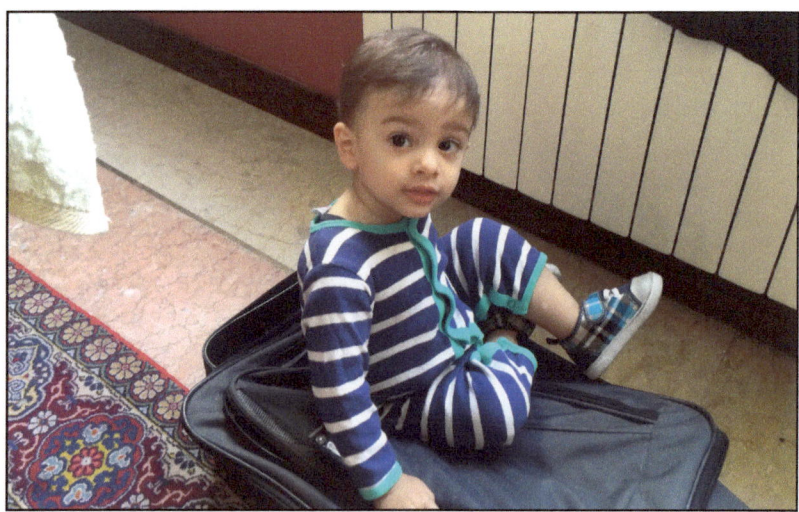

Taha likes sitting on my case

Wednesday 27 May

We had intended to set off early, but Farnaz had to sort out her visa application. She had decided to ask an agency, but she was dissatisfied with the service – the girl had made mistakes or had omitted things on the draft. They charge $100 on top of the $135 the application costs. The problem is they have her passport. She asked my opinion. I didn't know, but thought she should stick with the agency. Farnaz was upset, thinking I didn't trust to do the application online herself.

We pack the car quickly and grab stuff we might need to make tea – glass cups, a kettle, teabags. We also bunged in blankets and pillows, but no mattress. We set off.

It was complicated to find the right motorway because the slip road we wanted was closed. But we managed and headed south-east, parallel with the mountains but further south than last time, on the edge of the desert.

We are heading for a salt mine near Garmsar called Kuhdasht-e kohan. Ali Reza had said that there was a tricky section crossing wasteland to get from a highway to a parallel minor road. We try what looks like a well-used track but keep getting blocked by deep gullies or berms of rubble. At one point we attempt to descend a steep rough section to a dry riverbed. Farnaz asks me

Kuhdasht-e kohan salt mine

to get out and watch, but I think it is too soft and that we will never get back up. It is just as well since the riverbed is a dead end. Finally we get back to the highway try further on and find a way through.

We drove for about 10 km and stopped at a blockhouse where a tall deeply tanned man came out. Farnaz has rung him to arrange the visit. He climbed in the back and directed us up the steep track and into a narrow gorge that led to a deep cleft in the rock face.

There are tracks of heavy lorries and we drive on into the cavern. Inside it is huge, over 30m high and 20m broad. They have been working the mine for 18 years. They use air guns to drill into the relatively soft rock, lay charges and blow out a 3m deep section which they then load onto fleets of lorries with the JCBs we saw parked at the entrance.

There is a huge flexible duct running the length of the cavern that the man says brings fresh air in when the lorries are working. There is a heavy smell of carbon monoxide even though there have been no vehicles working for a while. The miners have left huge columns to support the roof and on the floor of the cavern there is a deep layer of salt. He says it's 95% pure. They take it to a factory in Garmsar. The owner has three or four mines but this is the biggest – the biggest mine in Asia, he says. We drive back. Farnaz asked me how much I want to give him. But he refuses the money. I try but again, he

Hotel Shahmizard

says no. Such a generous nature.

From here it's a long drive to Shahmizard where we plan to spend the night at a hotel the family have stayed at before. We buy more Red Bull. Then we are climbing towards the mountains. We try another large hotel first that Farnaz thinks she might like better. It looked good on the billboards at the entrance to the town but the manager is unfriendly and the two rooms he shows us are dingy. So we say we want to look at another hotel first further up the valley.

This one is a much nicer hotel, beautiful, small, well appointed and set around a courtyard garden. The rooms they show us are lovely! They have a flower theme in different colours. We're lucky we just clinch the deal when three people, who were also at the other hotel, arrive looking for rooms.

It's too late for dinner so we drive back into town to a huge restaurant. It has two massive empty banqueting halls under canvas. But the manager is behind a hatch and is on the telephone. Maybe they're full I say, joking. Finally I get bored waiting and suggest we try the small place we passed. We sit on a raised carpeted platform, take off our shoes and lounge back against the cushions. It's rice and chicken again. Luckily we have one plate between us and although we are hungry we still can't finish it all. It's relaxing lounging, but it's chilly and so we go back to the hotel.

Outdoor restaurant Shahmizard

Thursday 28 May

This is our big day to visit the salt-pans at Badab Soort. I have seen photos of these tiered limestone pools and I'm looking forward to seeing them. Breakfast is in a basement but the walls have been lined with small limestone bricks which, being white, make the place bright and welcoming. We are the first to breakfast – good bread and the usual soft cheese, fresh dates, honey. We sit in the garden under the trees and chat. We pack and go to the office to pay. I say I like their hotel. The wife smiles.

We drive into town to buy something for lunch and run into an Iranian professor from UCL. He is here for a conference on planning and heard us speaking English. We exchange contact details. He's very affable. Then we set off. It's a long beautiful drive through green rolling countryside.

We stop so Farnaz can telephone. She phoned while driving much of yesterday, trying to organise the visa with the agency and dictating corrections to the form. I made a gentle comment about not doing it if she had children in the car and she's taking it to heart. It's a nice place to stop. I sit on a rock and watch shepherds dividing a flock of wild looking sheep and driving half of them down into the green bottom fields.

Again we stop many times to ask direction. I like it. I get to meet so many people this way. We arrive at Badab Soort. I can see the long white streak of

Wild sheep being herded down from high pasture

white limestone on the hillside above where the run-off from the pools has run down the hillside. We negotiate a lift in the back of a blue pickup truck. The driver offers us a front seat, but Farnaz prefers to stand in the back, holding onto the cabin roof, laughing with pleasure. It's a bumpy ride, but fun.

We arrive. It's spectacular. We're lucky there are not too many people. A man on top of the hill blows whistle as I stray too near the pools. They have just started to protect them. I approve. We take lots of photos and cross behind the main pool to see from the other side. People are sitting round the dangling their feet in the water. We climb onto a rock sticking out into the lake to dangle our feet. My trousers get wet but they will dry. It's hot and sunny. A young man explains that this is a deep spring and throws a stone to show how the water mineral rich bubbles up from the deep. The water then cascades gently down the hillside forming terraced pools.

We get out food and picnic on the bread, cheese and yoghurt. After lunch we walk up the hillside to get a view from above and then make our way back on foot. We meet two young couples in a quarry and Farnaz climbs onto blocks to have a photograph taken. I tried climbing the steep quarry walls. There are two rough fissure lines and I straddle between them. Farnaz takes a trick shot that makes it appear I am much higher than I am. It's a pleasant track down. We use the loos in the parking and then set off again.

Badab Soort bumpy lorry ride

Badab Soort

We have one last treat – Lake Choret. It's north east of here on the way to the coast. We drive up to a small village and asked directions of a policeman. He's rather handsome and I can tell Farnaz likes him.

Badab Soort

Badab Soort spring

Climbing in quarry below

Ali Reza's sister suggested the itinerary. We leave the main road and head up into the hills. It's very rural – steep green fields of corn and hay – impossibly steep for machine and cut by hand with a short sickle. This is dairy country and most households make yoghurt and cheese.

There are more cars on the road than I expected and it turns out that it is a funeral for a young man as everyone is in black, the women are weeping and the cars have a photograph of him plastered on their rear windows.

We arrive in the village where we have arranged to meet our guide. He's been giving someone a lift on his motorbike. We buy eggs and a can of tuna for dinner. We are supposed to be staying in a chalet; I imagine a small Leveret Croft. Our guide arrives and we follow his lead. The road turns to a dirt track and then steeply uphill. Farnaz fails on the first attempt. Workmen building a house shout that we will never make it and should hire a car. She taps the wheel for a moment contemplating the climb, sucking her nail. Then she sets off with a roar and easily gets up.

We follow him at a breakneck speed. It's like a rally. Farnaz loves it. I try taking photographs out of the window but we're bouncing around so much I think they'll be blurred. Poor car, says Farnaz laughing. We would never have found it without our guide, she says. Finally we are there at the lake and come to a sharp stop next to his motorbike. You drive faster than anyone else I brought

Chasing after our guide

Lake Choret

here, he says smiling, and asks for water to slake his dry mouth. He brushes the dirt from his clothes. We should leave at seven before it's dark, he says.

We have an hour. The lake is strange – there is a loud din from hundreds of mating frogs and petrified trees poke out of the water. I wonder if it's artificial and has been made recently. Our guide says the water was much higher in spring and in winter, when the lake freezes, people skate.

We set off and walk to the end of the lake. People have set up camp in the woods and are starting fires and scavenging for wood. We find a tree trunk that overhangs the water and climb on and sit for a while. Farnaz is deeply exercised by Pooyan and wants to talk.

It's getting time to go so we take photos and walk back to the car. The guide has been helping campers carry gear, so we have time to make tea. We get out the stove and camp chairs and have a nice cup of tea overlooking the lake. It would be nice to camp here but we are going to his chalet.

We set off and after a few miles stop by the side of the track. There is a shepherd with a flock of sheep. Our guide pulls the top strand barbed wire off a rude fence and we clamber over and climb a small hill. The chalet is a tiny rough hut. There are lots of gaps between the planks making up the walls. This is the style here. Maybe for ventilation. There is a tin roof and the stove-pipe. He opens the rustic door. It's tiny, less than 2 m² square with a plain concrete

Lake Choret - brewing tea

Shepherd on his way home

floor. There should be a carpet, he says apologetically. I look at Farnaz. There is no water, no electricity. We'll give it a miss, I say. He's disappointed but we will pay him anyway. This is the very bottom rung of the Iranian tourist industry.

He guides us back to where we can't get lost and breaks a branch off a roadside tree bearing hard green fruit and proffers it through the window saying, even if we can't stay in his chalet he can give us fruit. He leaves us before I realise he's going. I feel bad – I didn't say goodbye, I'm disappointed I forgot to take a photograph of the chalet and wistful that we are leaving this rural idyll for civilisation and a hotel bed.

We drive north through the mountains and call in on the house the Mahdavis used to have. When I first came here there were less houses and the road was unmade and it was difficult to get materials here, she says. Like the house we visited last weekend, Abbas came here every week to supervise construction. I can't see much, it's dark. It's near another aunt's house. I ask if the aunt still uses it a lot. Farnaz says no. Abbas sold our house to their son-in-law's family, she says, but the daughter divorced and the aunt doesn't like going and seeing her son-in-law's parents with all the bad memories.

We drive on intending to stay in the large hotel the family used to use when they came here. But there is a wedding and they are full. Farnaz is tired from all the driving and nearly cries when the hotel receptionist tells us there is no

Mazandaran on way to Sari

room. The receptionist sees her distress and says there is another hotel in Sari an hour's drive away. So we set off again. It's hard to find. Despite this being a holiday area there are few hotels since most people have their own place or stay with friends. The hotel isn't as nice as the last one but we get rooms and picnic on the remains of lunch before getting to bed late.

Friday 29 May

This is our last day and we plan to drive back to Tehran in the morning and avoid the traffic. It turns out to be a good plan as Abbas says one of the three roads through the mountains – the one we took last week – is closed and all the traffic will be coming our way.

First we have breakfast. It is very good – the usual mix of things but we are hungry after eating little yesterday. We pack, pay and set off. The road is spectacular. The railway runs parallel to the road. The hills are steep, there is a lot of snow here in winter and I can see lines of vertical timber fencing that must be to stop avalanche sliding onto the tracks. There are signs of the old road with brick arch bridges and the famous Veresk bridge built by the last Shah.

We stop near the top of the pass to have lunch. It's not an immediately promising restaurant but it turns out to be better than my first impression. The food is very good – local green vegetable soup, chicken and rice and amazingly

Herding sheep

fizzy fermented dough, the yoghurt drink. Farnaz says Iman like it so we buy a bottle for him.

The drive has been very easy. There is little traffic. In a few hours this road will be clogged and the police will reduce traffic to a single lane to reduce accidents. But we sail along.

We pass Pardis on the eastern outskirts of Tehran. Farnaz says she came to a course at the University here. Wasn't it too far to come, I ask. No I loved it. I had just started driving and loved racing. All the boys complimented me on my driving. I took many chances and nearly died many times. One time we had just bought a new car. We were in town. Suddenly a car came out of a side street. I was going too fast to stop. I swerved and hit a concrete lamp-post. It cost a lot. What did your dad say? He said he was so glad I hadn't hurt myself. What a good father, I said.

Saturday 30 May
We had a nice family breakfast, Farnaz went to work, and I settled down at my desk. I really want to finish my chapter today before I go home. They have been chasing me and I'm two weeks late. But it is more work than I thought comparing six case studies.

Yogurt farm

I worked steadily till 11.30. I'm flipping between my chapter and something else when Word freezes. I try and rescue the document but although I think I've been saving as I worked I seem to have lost most of my work that morning. It's depressing. But I get a coffee and buckle down and redo it all. It doesn't take as long and I've caught up by lunchtime.

Nasrin makes a nice lunch. She's looking after Taha. He's been in and out of my room and he likes sitting on my case. I don't mind. He's very good. He eats lots of lunch and Nasrin and I communicate somehow. It's very pleasant. Then back to work sorting out the references and writing the conclusion. I also organise the images. Finally I'm done.

Farnaz comes home. She's upset she hasn't heard from Pooyan since last night. She was expecting a call. I decide to send off my chapter. I have another day but I have had enough of it.

Farnaz has planned a surprise party for Nasrin tonight. It's her birthday tomorrow. Farnaz tells her she wants to talk about something important and takes her out. We all rush to change. Abbas, Iman and I go together. Taha is rattling around on the back seat. I offer to hold him. Abbas says yes and stops the car so Iman can hand him over. I hold him tight. He's fine. We get to the coffee bar. It's nice. They have reserved a table for us. Ali Reza, Sanaz and

Birthday party in coffee bar in Pasdaran

Negrin, Farnaz's cousin are there already.

We chat and play with Negrin's new gold iPhone 6. She only got it an hour ago and is very pleased with it. Farnaz and Nasrin arrive. She is surprised and pleased. She thought Farnaz had wanted to talk about Pooyan and hadn't expected us all to be there. Sanaz has a cake and plants a candle on top that says happy birthday. Nesrin blows it out and begins to feed Taha cake. We take lots of photos and everyone is very happy. Abbas takes Taha outside to play. He loves going out and playing. Sanaz presents the cherry red necklace and bangle they have bought as Nasrin's present.

Abbas and I drive back. He wants to talk about Farnaz and Pooyan. He asked me what I'd do if I was her father. I laugh, and say I can't say, but I understand his concerns. He says it's a big problem. I've been so lucky to have such a close family, he says. We talk about the cost of living and how banks will only lend 5% of the value so you have to buy with cash. We compare costs here and in Cambridge. We talk about parking. I say we parked on the street in Cambridge. He says it would be dangerous in Tehran. We talk about daughters. He asked what I do if I was Farnaz's father. I say I found it hard when my daughter was young but I had to zip up even when I was really worried because I wanted her to feel like she could come to me for help if she ever

Nesrin's birthday

got into trouble. Abbas says he has to button up too. But he doesn't know about Pooyan. I say nothing.

We get a home everyone arrives and we sit down to dinner – two kinds of rice, two kinds of meat – the beef pomegranate stew Abbas made yesterday. I Skype Scharlie and she is able to talk to everyone. They ask after Jack and they are very friendly insisting on her coming to Iran soon.

We go to my room and I suddenly have the thought that maybe I am flying tonight. It's Saturday but I fly at 4 am on Sunday. Farnaz checks my paperwork and says yes. It is already 10 pm so I begin to pack and have a shower.

Everyone is a little shocked I'm going so suddenly. Nasrin brings dried berries as a present and tells to me about how to cook them – a spoon full of water, a little sugar, fry for a couple of minutes, mix with a little rice in saffron. They ring a taxi for me. It will come at 1.30am. Farnaz and I chat for an hour then it's time to go. Abbas has gone to bed but Nasrin is awake and very warm. Negrin wakes to say goodbye. Farnaz comes down in the lift to see me into the taxi. A smooth ride, the usual slow queues and I'm flying to Turkey. A six-hour layover when I write my journal and the final leg to Stansted and home.

Birthday party in Pasdaran

www.ingramcontent.com/pod-product-compliance
Lightning Source LLC
Chambersburg PA
CBHW042324150426
43192CB00001B/34